AF574469

Solar Power

BY LAURA PERDEW

Stride
An Imprint of The Child's World®
childsworld.com

Published by The Child's World®
800-599-READ • childsworld.com

Photography Credits
Photographs ©: Diyana Dimitrova/Shutterstock Images, cover, 1, 7; Lukasz Pawel Szczepanski/Shutterstock Images, 5; SL Photography/Shutterstock Images, 6; Dima Zel/Shutterstock Images, 9; Shutterstock Images, 10, 13, 15, 16, 17, 20, 21, 22; Red Line Editorial, 11; Coral Brunner/Shutterstock Images, 19; iStockphoto, 25; Roschetzky Photography/Shutterstock Images, 26, 28

ISBN Information
9781503864955 (Reinforced Library Binding)
9781503866010 (Portable Document Format)
9781503866850 (Online Multi-user eBook)
9781503867697 (Electronic Publication)

LCCN 2022939503

Printed in the United States of America

ABOUT THE AUTHOR

Laura Perdew is a mom, writing consultant, and author of more than 40 books for children. She lives and plays in Boulder, Colorado.

Contents

CHAPTER ONE

Capturing the Sun

Light from the Sun takes eight minutes to travel to Earth. That light has a lot of energy. In fact, within 90 minutes, enough of the Sun's energy strikes Earth to meet the world's yearly energy demands. This energy from the Sun is called solar energy.

Humans first used solar energy in the 600s BC. They used glass materials to help make fire. People tilted the glass so the Sun's light passed through it. They focused the light on a single point. The solar energy could be used to make flammable materials catch fire. In the 200s BC, the Greeks and Romans lit torches with mirrors. The mirrors focused the Sun's light on a single point. In China in 20 AD, mirrors were used to light torches, too.

People also used solar energy for warmth. Roman bathhouses had sunrooms. The windows faced south. Sunlight came into the rooms and warmed them.

The Sun is about 93 million miles (150 million km) from Earth.

Some cliff houses of the Ancestral Pueblo people can still be seen today.

In the 1200s, the Ancestral Puebloans used solar energy in what would later become the U.S. Southwest. They put their buildings on south-facing cliffs. These buildings captured the Sun's warmth. This was especially important during cold winters. In the 1700s, the first solar oven was made. It used reflected light to cook and heat food.

Today, **solar panels** are often used to catch the Sun's energy. A single solar panel has many photovoltaic (PV) cells on it. These are also known as solar cells. PV cells change light energy into electrical energy.

It took years to develop PV cells. A lot of scientists worked hard to make this happen. They made PV cells using different materials and chemicals over the years. It was not until the 1950s that the PV cells used today were created.

Rooftop solar panels can provide all the electricity a house needs.

In 1954, scientists at Bell Laboratories made PV cells with a material called silicon. Silicon PV cells are more efficient at converting sunlight than other materials.

Solar panels create electricity. Much of that electricity goes into the **electrical grid**. It powers homes, schools, hospitals, and businesses. Smaller solar panels make this power available for other uses. Solar power can be used for things such as calculators and watches. It is used to power streetlights and signs. Solar hot water systems are used in some homes and businesses. And scientists are creating solar-powered products for cars and airplanes. Solar power is even used in space. For example, satellites and the International Space Station are powered by the Sun.

Solar power is an unlimited energy source. That means it will never run out. Solar power has the potential to meet all energy needs on Earth. And solar power is clean. Unlike **fossil fuels**, solar power does not give off harmful gases that contribute to **climate change**.

The International Space Station uses huge solar panels to make electricity.

Using solar power more and more can help fight climate change. Scientists are creating the technology to improve efficiency and lower costs. The goal is for solar energy to help power the future.

CHAPTER TWO

How Solar Energy Works

There are two types of solar energy: passive and active. Passive solar energy has been used for thousands of years. It requires no technology. Instead, it uses only natural sunlight to warm buildings.

Many modern homes are designed to take advantage of passive solar energy. They might use active solar energy, too.

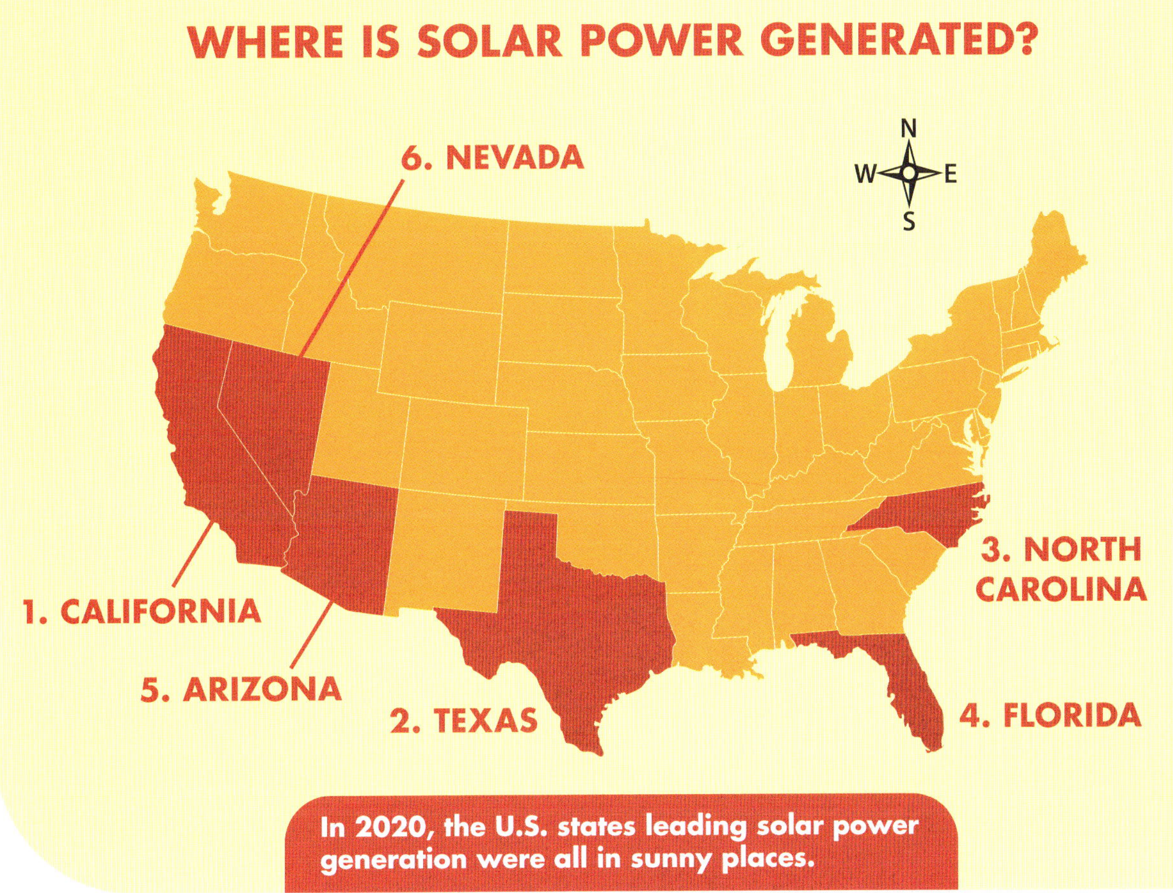

In 2020, the U.S. states leading solar power generation were all in sunny places.

Today, some buildings use passive solar energy. Some buildings in the northern part of the world are made with windows that face south. Those windows get the most direct sunlight all year. The buildings also use materials that absorb and hold heat. These materials include stone, tile, brick, and concrete. Also, the buildings are made so air flows easily through the interior. Some buildings have fans to move the warmed air.

Unlike passive solar energy, active solar energy needs technology to work. PV cells made of silicon are one of the most common ways to capture solar energy today. Many PV cells together make up a solar panel. Many solar panels together are called an array. To make electricity, the Sun shines on the panels. The panels absorb the energy from the sunlight. The energy is converted into usable electricity. Wires are connected to the system. They deliver the electricity to homes and buildings.

SOLAR CAR RACE

The first solar car race was held in 1985. In Switzerland, drivers raced solar cars to raise awareness for PV systems. Four years later, the first American Tour de Sol took place. There is also a race across Australia that happens every two years. These events encourage solar developments. And they show that the Sun can power cars.

Another type of active solar energy is concentrated solar power (CSP). Instead of panels, CSP uses mirrors. These mirrors focus sunlight to heat a fluid. The heated fluid is then used to make electricity. Sometimes it is stored to use later. CSP is most often used for large-scale power stations.

A CSP power plant in Spain uses a huge field of mirrors that focuses light on a central point.

Both active and passive solar systems help meet energy demands. Because of its many benefits, the use of solar power is growing.

CHAPTER THREE

Benefits of Solar Energy

The Sun is a renewable resource. Renewable resources are natural sources of energy. They will never run out. Earth has an endless supply of sunlight. In addition, solar power is a source of clean energy. It does not burn fossil fuels. It does not give off harmful gases that lead to climate change. Solar power itself does not **pollute** the air or water. For instance, there is no chance of this energy source spilling into the ocean and polluting it, like oil could. In addition, solar power does not pose a risk of a dangerous gas leak, like natural gas does. Using solar power lowers the human impact on the environment.

After solar power systems are set up, they are easy to take care of. This is because there are no moving parts that can wear out. A system can last decades.

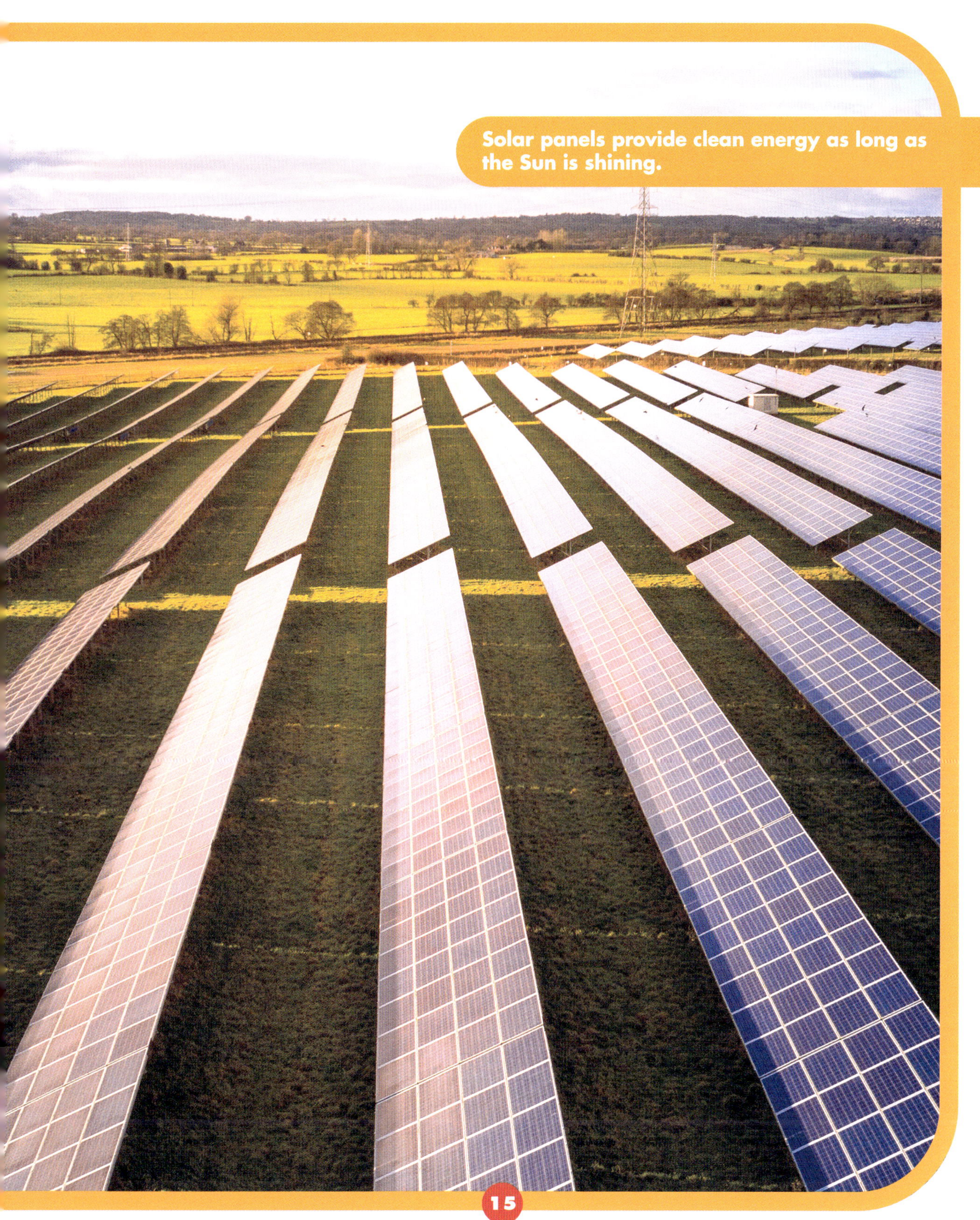

Solar panels provide clean energy as long as the Sun is shining.

SOLAR OVENS

Approximately three billion people around the world use open fires to cook food. This may lead to health problems, the destruction of forests, and climate change. It also keeps many people from going to school. That is because they are forced to spend their days collecting wood to burn. Solar-powered ovens are a clean alternative. They use mirrors to focus sunlight on a small area to cook food. The stoves do not give off harmful gases. They are safe and reliable.

Also, these systems do not make any noise. They do not need fossil fuels to work. They simply need the Sun.

Another benefit of solar power is lower electric bills. Once installed, solar systems make power for free. Sometimes solar systems even make more electricity than is needed. When that happens, the electricity returns to the electrical grid. Home and building owners are then paid for this excess electricity. Plus, solar power protects people from rising fuel prices.

Fuel prices may go up, but making solar power remains free. At the same time, solar helps the United States make its own power. Sunlight does not need to be brought in from another country like some fossil fuels. With solar, the United States does not need to rely on other countries for fuel. Using solar energy lets individuals, businesses, states, and countries be energy independent.

The solar industry has another positive impact. As it grows, it creates jobs. People are needed to research, make, move, and install solar power systems. In 2021, the solar industry employed more than 260,000 people. By 2035, that number could be more than one million.

The solar industry is growing quickly, creating many new jobs.

CHAPTER FOUR

Drawbacks to Solar Energy

One of the limitations of solar energy is cost. Buying and installing an array is expensive. For homeowners, the up-front cost is often too much. Also, putting in an array requires space. Sometimes arrays are placed on rooftops. Larger arrays are put in fields. For example, the Agua Caliente Solar Project in Arizona has 4.9 million PV panels. It makes enough electricity to power 100,000 homes. But it takes up 2,400 acres (970 ha) of land. That is more than 1,800 football fields side by side.

Solar power has environmental impacts, too. For example, the land needed for large-scale arrays must be cleared. Clearing natural areas breaks large **habitats** into smaller and smaller pieces. And smaller habitats harm plant and animal populations.

Large solar farms take up a lot of space.

In addition, some solar power systems need to be cleaned or cooled. These processes use a lot of water. This affects water resources, especially in dry areas.

Building solar panels takes a significant amount of energy.

Other environmental impacts happen when people make or throw away solar panels. A lot of energy is needed to make solar power systems. Much of that energy is made by using fossil fuels. Plus, solar panels are made from **toxic** materials. If not properly thrown away, old solar panels could leak these toxic chemicals into the environment. All of these things affect plants, animals, and humans.

Even small solar panels need to be carefully thrown away.

In cold areas, snow may get on solar panels.

Another drawback of solar energy is that it depends on the Sun. At nighttime or on cloudy days, solar power systems cannot make electricity. Similarly, solar production is affected by the time of year, and it changes depending on location. For example, in the northern part of the world, solar power generation is greatest between March and October. During the winter months, less energy is made. Storing energy created by the Sun has also been a challenge. Batteries that store solar power are expensive. And storage can be difficult for large-scale systems. That is why most homes and businesses are still connected to the electrical grid. Much of the grid's power is made using fossil fuels. People are staying connected to the electrical grid because they are able to access power from it even when the Sun is not out.

In spite of these challenges, the Sun has the potential to meet all energy needs on Earth. Therefore, scientists and engineers are working hard. They want to improve solar energy for everyone.

CHAPTER FIVE

Into the Future

To slow climate change, clean energy is replacing fossil fuels. In 2021, only 3 percent of the energy made in the United States came from solar power. But by 2050, solar energy could supply 45 percent of the electricity in the United States. It can be paired with other sources of clean energy, too. This could include hydropower, which is power from water, and wind power. Together, these sources could provide reliable, renewable energy.

One key to a renewable energy future is putting solar panels on more buildings. To encourage this, some governments give solar tax credits. That means people can get financial help to put in solar panels. For example, in 2022 homeowners in the United States could save 26 percent on the cost of a solar power system. Some states offer additional credits. Also, the up-front cost of solar power systems has gone down over the years.

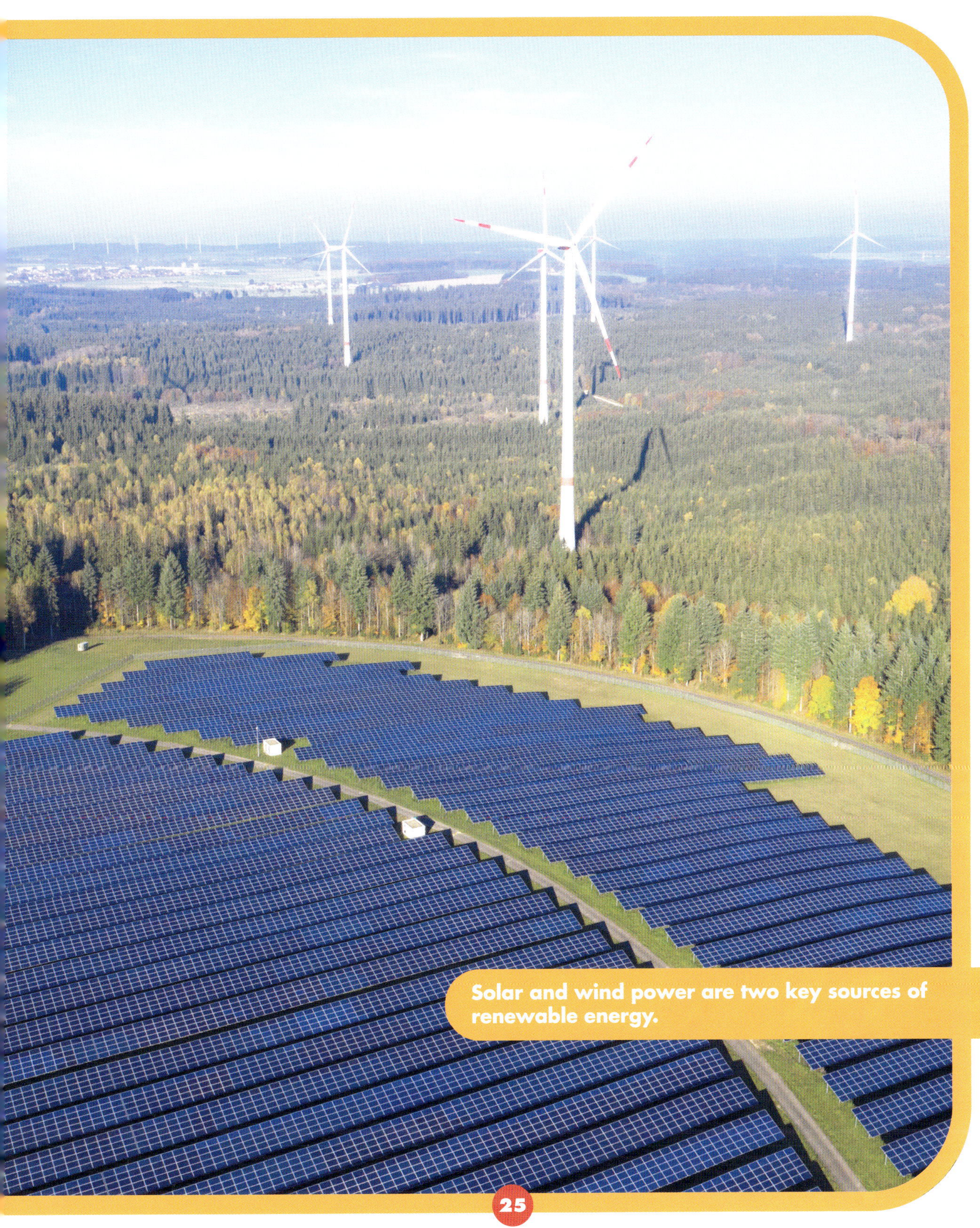

Solar and wind power are two key sources of renewable energy.

Large batteries, including those made by the car company Tesla, can store electricity from solar panels. Then the batteries can release the power when it is needed.

Between 2000 and 2019, the cost of solar decreased by 50 percent. Slowly, solar power systems are becoming more affordable for more people.

Research is making solar panels more efficient, too. A more efficient panel will be able to capture more energy from the Sun. As a result, smaller arrays will make the same amount of energy. Energy storage improvements will help as well. The energy made by the Sun can then be available at all times.

Other advances in solar technology include solar windows, roof tiles, and paint. Solar windows look like regular windows. They are see-through. The only difference is that solar windows capture sunlight and change it into electricity. Another alternative to large solar panels is solar roof tiles. These roof tiles take the place of traditional shingles. They are made of sheets of thin PV cells.

SOLAR AIRPLANES

Engineers are creating solar-powered airplanes. In 2016, a solar-powered plane flew around the world. It did not use any fossil fuels. The plane had more than 17,000 thin PV cells on its wings and body. It had four batteries for power storage.

Solar power will be an important part of the world's clean energy future.

Just like the larger panels, they change sunlight into electricity. Not only are they similar in size to traditional shingles, but they are also more efficient than panels. Roofs with solar tiles look just like roofs with shingles. Solar paint is another technology, but people are still working on it. The goal is to create a paint that looks like regular paint but also generates electricity.

Solar technology is always improving. Costs are going down. More people are putting in solar power systems. As a result, the Sun will help keep the world powered into the future.

Glossary

climate change (KLYE-mit CHAYNJ) Climate change refers to long-term changes in global temperature and weather patterns. Greenhouse gases released by fossil fuels can lead to climate change.

electrical grid (eh-LEK-tri-kuhl GRID) The electrical grid is the system that produces and delivers electricity to users. When solar panels produce more electricity than a building needs, the excess electricity goes to the electrical grid.

fossil fuels (FOSS-uhl FYOO-uhls) Fossil fuels are sources of energy that come from the remains of plants and animals that died long ago. Coal, oil, and natural gas are examples of fossil fuels.

habitats (HAB-ih-tats) Habitats are places where plants and animals typically grow and live. Clearing land for solar panels can harm habitats.

pollute (puh-LOOT) To pollute means to contaminate something or make it dirty. Fossil fuels pollute the air.

solar panels (SOH-lur PAN-uhls) Solar panels are made up of solar cells that turn the energy from the Sun into electrical energy. Solar panels create clean energy for homes, schools, hospitals, and businesses.

toxic (TAHK-sik) Something that is toxic is poisonous. Toxic chemicals can hurt the environment.

Fast Facts

- The Sun gives Earth a lot of energy. People capture that energy and change it into electricity.
- Solar power is a renewable resource. It provides clean energy to people.
- Solar power can be expensive to install. It also has environmental impacts. For instance, clearing land for solar panels can hurt animal and plant habitats.
- The future of solar energy is bright. Scientists are developing technology to make solar power more efficient and less expensive.

One Stride Further

- Think about and list the ways you use passive solar energy in your daily life. How can you use passive solar energy more?
- How do you think the invention of active solar energy technology has helped people? How do you think it will help in the future?
- Do you think the positives of using solar power outweigh the negatives? Explain.
- Solar technology is improving every day. Imagine all the ways solar power might be used in the future. Write a short story about a future world that uses solar power in new and unexpected ways.

Find Out More

IN THE LIBRARY

Brearley, Laurie. *Solar Power: Capturing the Sun's Energy*. New York, NY: Children's Press, 2019.

Scibilia, Jade Zora. *Solar Panels: Harnessing the Power of the Sun*. New York, NY: PowerKids Press, 2018.

Swanson, Jennifer. *How Does Solar Energy Work?* Mankato, MN: The Child's World, 2022.

ON THE WEB

Visit our website for links about solar power: **childsworld.com/links**

Note to Parents, Teachers, and Librarians: We routinely verify our Web links to make sure they are safe and active sites. So encourage your readers to check them out!

Index